A Lamp to My Feet

An 11 week study in Psalm 119

Ron Wolfe

Contents

Introduction

In 1981, God graciously brought a man named Lloyd Jonas into my life. Lloyd was a pastor at a church about 25 miles from where I was pastoring on Cape Cod. He invited me to biblical counseling training that he was conducting at his church and, after three invitations, I reluctantly agreed. It turned out to be a life-changing experience. Since then, I've lost count of the people I've had the privilege to counsel.

One of my convictions has been that many of the problems we face, whether due to our sinful choices or the sinful choices of others, stem from having a low view of God and the sufficiency of His Word. In 2 Corinthians 3:18, we read, "And we all, with unveiled face, beholding the glory of the Lord, are being transformed into the same image from one degree of glory to another. For this comes from the Lord who is the Spirit." This workbook has been developed not only to address the immediate problems our counselees bring but also to create a devotional tool that will direct their focus toward God. This will increase their faith and trust in God and His Word. Not only for their salvation accomplished by the substitutionary death of Christ on the cross but the ongoing transformation into the image of Christ. Which will help them address their present issues and develop a stronger reliance on God's Word that can prevent future decisions that may lead to repeated habits of sin and painful consequences.

A powerful example of the sufficiency of God's Word is Psalm 119, the longest chapter in the Bible, consisting of 176 verses. It is an acrostic poem, with each section beginning with a successive letter of the Hebrew alphabet. The psalm is a meditation on the greatness of God and importance of His Word. It is believed to be written by David, possibly towards the end of his life, and it reflects his deep love and reverence for God's commandments. The psalm is divided into 22 parts, and each part contains eight verses. This structure was likely intended to aid in memorization and to emphasize the completeness and perfection of God's Word.

Purpose of This Book

This book is designed to serve as a comprehensive homework manual for biblical counseling. It can additionally be a valuable resource for small groups or an individual study of Psalm 119, helping readers to delve deeply into its rich and profound teachings.

The central purpose of this book is to emphasize the majesty of God and the absolute necessity and value of His Word. It aims to highlight the wisdom that the Scriptures provide for all aspects of life and worship. By continually guiding the reader to the sufficiency of God's Word, this book seeks to offer more than just solutions to immediate problems but also to provide a foundation for sound decision-making in the future.

Structure

The book is divided into eleven sections, each corresponding to parts of Psalm 119. It is meant to be used over eleven weeks, but can be read at your own pace. Each section includes:

- Reading: Sixteen verses of Psalm 119, intended to be read twice a day.

- Themes: Representative themes drawn from the verses, focusing on the behaviors and results of obedient living.

- Reflection and Application: Concluding questions that prompt reflection and practical application of the text to the individual's daily life.

Application

In the context of biblical counseling, the purpose of this book is to elevate the eyes of the counselee to the majesty and sufficiency of God's Word for all of life, not just the present issues they face. The book encourages a deeper reliance on Scripture, fostering a holistic and preventative approach to personal growth and decision-making. The accumulation of God's wisdom through regular reflection and application can help in making better choices in the future.

It can also be used in a small group allowing for personal study and then discussion within the group context or one's own Bible study. In all of these uses, the goal is the same, to elevate ones view and understanding of God and the sufficiency of His revelation in the written Word.

In summary, this book is not only a tool for addressing immediate needs but also a guide for cultivating a lifelong habit of scriptural reflection and application, ensuring that the wisdom of God infuses every aspect of the reader's life.

Acknowledgements

I want to acknowledge several people who have been instrumental in this project. Bryan Lamb, a pastor, fellow counselor, and great friend from Los Angeles, offered many valuable thoughts on the goals of this homework manual. Another key contributor is Joshua Chadd, who assisted with the formatting, structure, and publishing of this project. Additional thanks to Mary Ann and Jon Corombos for helpful guidance in the editing process. I also want to thank the congregation of Redemption Hill church in Kingsford, MI. It has been my privilege to serve this wonderful church since 1991. This group of people has caused me to grow in ways neither of us could have imagined. God used them over the years to expose my own heart and my constant need of God's grace and wisdom to serve them as an under shepherd of Jesus.

Lastly, I want to thank my wife Joan for her encouragement and companionship over nearly six decades. She has been a steady support when the challenges of life and ministry have been intense. When I read Proverbs 31, her name is constantly on my mind. To the broader community of biblical counseling to whom I owe great gratitude because all of this is to the glory of God, our Creator, Redeemer, and Friend.

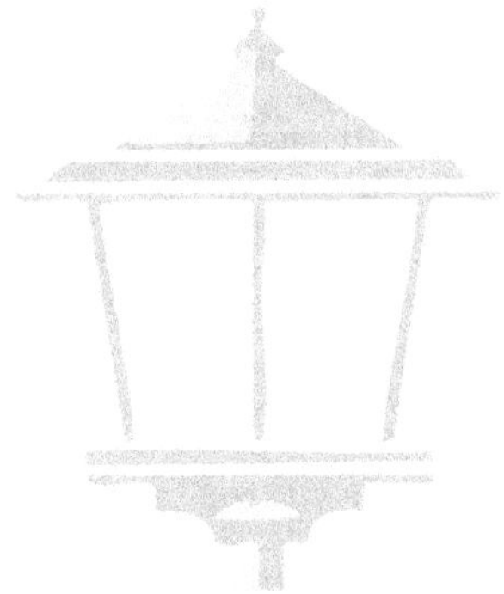

Psalm 119:1-16

"Blessed are those whose way is blameless,
who walk in the law of the Lord!
Blessed are those who keep his testimonies,
who seek him with their whole heart,
who also do no wrong,
but walk in his ways!
You have commanded your precepts
to be kept diligently.
Oh that my ways may be steadfast
in keeping your statutes!

Then I shall not be put to shame,

having my eyes fixed on all your commandments.

I will praise you with an upright heart,

when I learn your righteous rules.

I will keep your statutes;

do not utterly forsake me!

How can a young man keep his way pure?

By guarding it according to your word.

With my whole heart I seek you;

let me not wander from your commandments!

I have stored up your word in my heart,

that I might not sin against you.

Blessed are you, O Lord;

teach me your statutes!

With my lips I declare

all the rules of your mouth.

In the way of your testimonies I delight

as much as in all riches.

I will meditate on your precepts

and fix my eyes on your ways.

I will delight in your statutes;

I will not forget your word."

Psalm 119:1-16

Read Psalm 119:1-16, twice daily

Summary: The psalmist describes the blessed or happy state of those who live blamelessly and walk in the law of the Lord. These individuals hate sin, seeking to avoid it and follow God's ways without hypocrisy. He acknowledges God's command to be strenuous in keeping His precepts and expresses a sincere desire for consistent obedience. The righteous will not be put to shame when they live in obedience to God's Word. They commit to praising God with a pure heart as they learn His righteous laws. The psalmist pleads with God not to forsake him, acknowledging his total dependence on God.

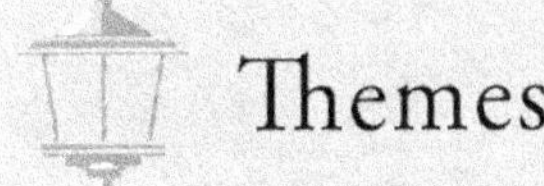# Themes

Obedient believers:

- Are blessed with happiness and true joy.

- Diligently strive to obey God's Word without hypocrisy.

- Seek to walk blamelessly, hating sin and avoiding it.

- Acknowledge their need for God's presence and enabling power to live obediently and righteously.

- Study, meditate, and memorize God's Word to avoid sin.

- Faithfully worship, praise, and desire God's instruction.

- Find joy and delight in obeying God's Word comparing it to finding great riches.

 # Questions for Reflection

Please list five qualities these verses reflect about God.

1.

2.

3.

4.

5.

What practical steps can you take to know God wholeheartedly that will keep you from straying away from Him?

____

____

____

____

____

____

How does God's Word affect your actions and decisions?

____

____

____

____

____

What sins might hinder you from experiencing joy? How can you rely on God's presence and enabling power to overcome them?

____

____

____

____

____

Do you identify with the psalmist's request for steadfastness, sharing the struggle Paul reflects in Romans 7:15-23? If so, how?

____

____

____

____

____

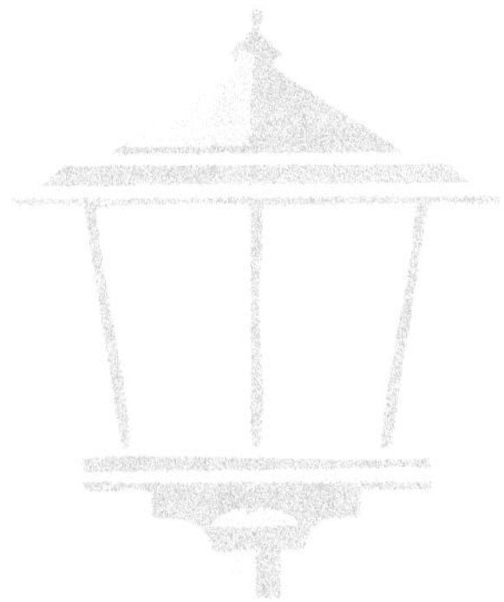

Psalm 119:17-32

"Deal bountifully with your servant,
that I may live and keep your word.
Open my eyes, that I may behold
wondrous things out of your law.
I am a sojourner on the earth;
hide not your commandments from me!
My soul is consumed with longing
for your rules at all times.
You rebuke the insolent, accursed ones,
who wander from your commandments.

Take away from me scorn and contempt,

for I have kept your testimonies.

Even though princes sit plotting against me,

your servant will meditate on your statutes.

Your testimonies are my delight;

they are my counselors.

My soul clings to the dust;

give me life according to your word!

When I told of my ways, you answered me;

teach me your statutes!

Make me understand the way of your precepts,

and I will meditate on your wondrous works.

My soul melts away for sorrow;

strengthen me according to your word!

Put false ways far from me

and graciously teach me your law!

I have chosen the way of faithfulness;

I set your rules before me.

I cling to your testimonies, O Lord;

let me not be put to shame!

I will run in the way of your commandments

when you enlarge my heart!"

Psalm 119:17-32

Read Psalm 119:17-32, twice daily

Summary: The psalmist expresses a need and desire for God's grace so he can live and obey God's commands, acknowledging he is a stranger on earth in need of divine direction, asking God to open his eyes to the wonders of His law, and expressing love and delight in God's commandments. He also addresses the contempt and opposition he faces from others, asking for relief and reaffirming his commitment to meditate on God's statutes. The commandments are a delight to his soul, and they have become his counselors and source of wisdom. The psalmist expresses a deep sense of humility and desperation, pleading that God would help guide and revive him according to His word. He concludes by expressing his determination to obey God, seeking not to be put to shame.

 ## Themes

Obedient believers:

- Acknowledge their complete dependence on God for understanding life itself.

- Have a strong desire to comprehend and obey God's laws.

- See themselves as a "sojourners or strangers," highlighting the temporary nature of life and the need for God's enduring word.

- Have a deep love and appreciation for God's commandments because while they will encounter rejection, they are instructed to seek refuge in God's Word.

- Acknowledge their own insufficiency and turn to God for revival and strength.

- Admit their own sin and seek forgiveness from God.

- Hate and struggle against sin, recognizing the deceitfulness of it and the need for God's help to overcome it.

Questions for Reflection

Please list five qualities these verses reflect about God.

1.

2.

3.

4.

5.

Do you see your own dependence on God in your daily life? Explain why or why not.

____

____

____

____

____

How does recognizing life as temporary influence your priorities and actions?

____

____

____

____

____

How does God's Word provide you with strength and courage when you face opposition to your faith?

____

____

____

____

____

Do you ever feel the desperation of the psalmist? If so, what do you request of God in those times?

____

____

____

____

____

____

Psalm 119:33-48

"Teach me, O Lord, the way of your statutes;
and I will keep it to the end.
Give me understanding, that I may keep your law
and observe it with my whole heart.
Lead me in the path of your commandments,
for I delight in it.
Incline my heart to your testimonies,
and not to selfish gain!
Turn my eyes from looking at worthless things;
and give me life in your ways.

Confirm to your servant your promise,

that you may be feared.

Turn away the reproach that I dread,

for your rules are good.

Behold, I long for your precepts;

in your righteousness give me life!

Let your steadfast love come to me, O Lord,

your salvation according to your promise;

then shall I have an answer for him who taunts me,

for I trust in your word.

And take not the word of truth utterly out of my mouth,

for my hope is in your rules.

I will keep your law continually,

forever and ever,

and I shall walk in a wide place,

for I have sought your precepts.

I will also speak of your testimonies before kings

and shall not be put to shame,

for I find my delight in your commandments,

which I love.

I will lift up my hands toward your commandments, which

I love,

and I will meditate on your statutes."

Psalm 119:33-48

Read Psalm 119:33-48, twice daily

Summary: The psalmist is committed to God's laws and decrees. He asks God to teach him His statutes, give him understanding, and lead him in righteousness. He delights in God's statutes and turns away from worthless things, finding true joy in God's ways, praying for God's unfailing love and salvation. He trusts God's Word and speaks of it without shame.

 ## Themes

Obedient believers:

- Desire God's teaching and wisdom.

- Commit to obey God's commands.

- Thank God for His steadfast love and faithfulness, which are the foundations of trust and hope.

- Seek transformation through the power of God's Word, asking for strength to turn away from sin and worthless pursuits.

- Speak boldly about God's commands, indicating confidence in the righteousness of God's Word.

Questions for Reflection

Please list five qualities these verses reflect about God.

1.

2.

3.

4.

5.

How can you develop a desire for God's Word and guidance daily?

____

____

____

____

____

In what areas do you struggle to follow God's commands?
List three:

1.

2.

3.

How have you experienced God's steadfast love and faithfulness? How does this impact your trust in His promises?

____

____

____

____

____

What "worthless things" distract you from pursuing God's ways?
List three:

1.

2.

3.

In what situations do you hesitate to speak about your faith?

____

____

____

____

How can you gain the confidence to share God's Word more boldly?

____

____

____

____

____

Psalm 119:49-64

"Remember your word to your servant,
in which you have made me hope.
This is my comfort in my affliction,
that your promise gives me life.
The insolent utterly deride me,
but I do not turn away from your law.
When I think of your rules from of old,
I take comfort, O Lord.
Hot indignation seizes me because of the wicked,
who forsake your law.

Your statutes have been my songs

in the house of my sojourning.

I remember your name in the night, O Lord,

and keep your law.

This blessing has fallen to me,

that I have kept your precepts.

The Lord is my portion;

I promise to keep your words.

I entreat your favor with all my heart;

be gracious to me according to your promise.

When I think on my ways,

I turn my feet to your testimonies;

I hasten and do not delay

to keep your commandments.

Though the cords of the wicked ensnare me,

I do not forget your law.

At midnight I rise to praise you,

because of your righteous rules.

I am a companion of all who fear you,

of those who keep your precepts.

The earth, O Lord, is full of your steadfast love;

teach me your statutes!"

Psalm 119:49-64

Read Psalm 119:49-64, twice daily

Summary: Dependence on God's promises provides comfort during suffering and opposition. The psalmist is committed to God's Word and desires divine instruction. He is determined to follow God's commands. Despite the mocking of the arrogant, he remains devoted to God's commands. He praises God's name, declares God to be his portion, and vows to obey God's commands. He desires God's blessing and requests mercy. The psalmist highlights the earth's fullness of God's love and grace by expressing companionship with those who fear God.

 Themes

Obedient believers:

- Trust God's promises for hope and comfort.

- Run to God for comfort during difficult times of suffering.

- Have an unwavering commitment to God's laws and statutes.

- Evaluate their commitment to God's ways and look for evidence of fruit.

- Benefit from community and fellowship with other believers.

- Become aware of the need and value of corporate praise and worship.

- Consistently praise God and meditate on His righteous laws despite circumstances.

 # Questions for Reflection

Please list five qualities these verses reflect about God.

1.

2.

3.

4.

5.

What specific promises from God bring you comfort? How do they impact you?

____

____

____

____

____

How can you apply more of God's Word into your daily life to find ongoing comfort and guidance?

____

____

____

____

____

Are there areas in your life where you struggle to remain devoted to God's commands? How can you address these struggles?

____

____

____

____

____

What practices can you implement to ensure regular self-examination and repentance?

____

____

____

____

____

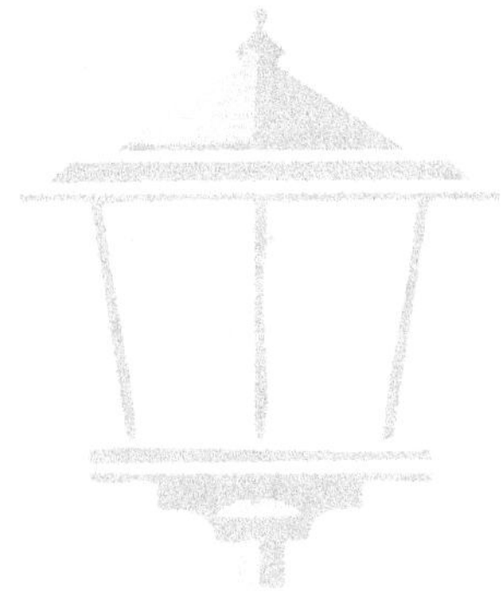

Psalm 119:65-80

"You have dealt well with your servant,
O Lord, according to your word.
Teach me good judgment and knowledge,
for I believe in your commandments.
Before I was afflicted I went astray,
but now I keep your word.
You are good and do good;
teach me your statutes.
The insolent smear me with lies,
but with my whole heart I keep your precepts;

their heart is unfeeling like fat,

but I delight in your law.

It is good for me that I was afflicted,

that I might learn your statutes.

The law of your mouth is better to me

than thousands of gold and silver pieces.

Your hands have made and fashioned me;

give me understanding that I may learn your

commandments.

Those who fear you shall see me and rejoice,

because I have hoped in your word.

I know, O Lord, that your rules are righteous,

and that in faithfulness you have afflicted me.

Let your steadfast love comfort me

according to your promise to your servant.

Let your mercy come to me, that I may live;

for your law is my delight.

Let the insolent be put to shame,

because they have wronged me with falsehood;

as for me, I will meditate on your precepts.

Let those who fear you turn to me,

that they may know your testimonies.

May my heart be blameless in your statutes,

that I may not be put to shame!"

Psalm 119:65-80

Read Psalm 119:65-80, twice daily

Summary: The psalmist reflects on God's faithfulness and the value of His commandments. He acknowledges the goodness and righteousness of God's laws and expresses a desire to learn and obey them. He admits past sins and recognizes that affliction has led to a deeper understanding of God's statutes. He also trusts God to deliver and comfort, emphasizing the importance of God's precepts in guiding life.

 ## Themes

Obedient believers:

- Acknowledge that God is good and does good, reflecting trust in God's character and actions.

- Know the importance of God's commandments, statutes, and precepts, highlighting their role in guiding, teaching, and providing wisdom for life.

- See affliction as a means of learning and growth, indicating that suffering brings a greater understanding and appreciation of God's laws.

- Have a desire to understand and follow God's commandments.

- Trust in God's promise to deliver and provide comfort in times of difficulty.

Questions for Reflection

Please list five qualities these verses reflect about God.

1.

2.

3.

4.

5.

Has knowing and following God's commandments led to a more consistent godly walk in your life? In what ways has it done so?

____

____

____

____

____

How have challenges and afflictions provided spiritual growth and a deeper understanding of God's will?

____

____

____

____

____

Do you actively seek to understand and live by divine principles? How does this shape your character and actions?

____

____

____

____

____

Psalm 119:81-96

"My soul longs for your salvation;
I hope in your word.
My eyes long for your promise;
I ask, "When will you comfort me?"
For I have become like a wineskin in the smoke,
yet I have not forgotten your statutes.
How long must your servant endure?
When will you judge those who persecute me?
The insolent have dug pitfalls for me;
they do not live according to your law.

All your commandments are sure;

they persecute me with falsehood; help me!

They have almost made an end of me on earth,

but I have not forsaken your precepts.

In your steadfast love give me life,

that I may keep the testimonies of your mouth.

Forever, O Lord, your word

is firmly fixed in the heavens.

Your faithfulness endures to all generations;

you have established the earth, and it stands fast.

By your appointment they stand this day,

for all things are your servants.

If your law had not been my delight,

I would have perished in my affliction.

I will never forget your precepts,

for by them you have given me life.

I am yours; save me,

for I have sought your precepts.

The wicked lie in wait to destroy me,

but I consider your testimonies.

I have seen a limit to all perfection,

but your commandment is exceedingly broad."

Psalm 119:81-96

Read Psalm 119:81-96, twice daily

Summary: This passage expresses a deep desire and dependence on God's Word during times of distress. The psalmist describes his soul fainting for salvation, trusting in God's promises, while suffering at the hands of his enemies. Despite struggles, he remains firm in his trust of God's commandments. The passage concludes with a reaffirmation of God's faithfulness and the limitless nature of His commands.

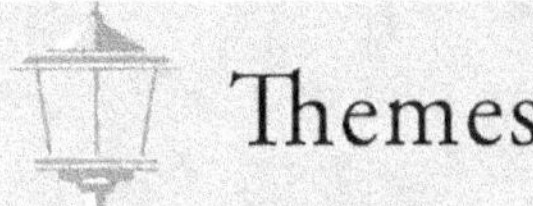 Themes

Obedient Believers:

- Long for God's salvation with intense desire for God's deliverance and reassurance through His word.

- Remain committed to God's statutes, even in hardship and oppression.

- Trust God's promises.

- Recognize that human efforts have limitations, but God's word is boundless.

 # Questions for Reflection

Please list five qualities these verses reflect about God.

1.

2.

3.

4.

5.

Have you ever experienced a deep desire for God's presence and guidance in times of distress? How did you respond?

____

____

____

____

____

How does your faith help you to endure suffering and uncertainty?

____

____

____

____

____

In what ways do you see God's faithfulness reflected in your life?

How does knowing that God's word is limitless change the way you approach Scripture and your relationship with Him?

What practical steps can you take to trust God's word more deeply, especially in challenging seasons?

Psalm 119:97-112

"Oh how I love your law!
It is my meditation all the day.
Your commandment makes me wiser than my enemies,
for it is ever with me.
I have more understanding than all my teachers,
for your testimonies are my meditation.
I understand more than the aged,
for I keep your precepts.
I hold back my feet from every evil way,
in order to keep your word.

I do not turn aside from your rules,

for you have taught me.

How sweet are your words to my taste,

sweeter than honey to my mouth!

Through your precepts I get understanding;

therefore I hate every false way.

Your word is a lamp to my feet

and a light to my path.

I have sworn an oath and confirmed it,

to keep your righteous rules.

I am severely afflicted;

give me life, O Lord, according to your word!

Accept my freewill offerings of praise, O Lord,

and teach me your rules.

I hold my life in my hand continually,

but I do not forget your law.

The wicked have laid a snare for me,

but I do not stray from your precepts.

Your testimonies are my heritage forever,

for they are the joy of my heart.

I incline my heart to perform your statutes

forever, to the end."

Psalm 119:97-112

Read Psalm 119:97-112, twice daily

Summary: This section emphasizes love for God's law and the wisdom it provides. The psalmist meditates on it continually and acknowledges that it makes him wiser than his enemies, teachers, and elders. He commits to following God's commands, avoiding sin, and staying on the right path. God's word is a lamp to his feet, guiding his steps. Despite affliction and hardship, he remains devoted to God's statutes and promises to follow them to the end.

Themes

Obedient believers:

- Express satisfaction in meditating on God's word, showing deep love and commitment to it.

- Discover that obedience to God's commands provides greater understanding than that of enemies, teachers, or elders.

- Value God's word as a guiding light that leads them on the right path, preventing them from wandering.

- Choose to remain faithful, even during difficult times, leaning on God's promises for strength.

- Actively choose to follow God's commands and keep them close to their heart.

Questions for Reflection

Please list five qualities these verses reflect about God.

1.

2.

3.

4.

5.

How does meditating on God's word influence your daily decisions and attitudes?

____

____

____

____

____

In what ways has following God's teachings given you wisdom beyond human understanding?

____

____

____

____

____

How do you rely on God's word for guidance in difficult situations?

When facing trials, do you find it easy or difficult to stay committed to God's commands? Why?

What practical steps can you take to make Scripture a consistent source of wisdom and direction in your life?

Psalm 119:113-128

"I hate the double-minded,
but I love your law.
You are my hiding place and my shield;
I hope in your word.
Depart from me, you evildoers,
that I may keep the commandments of my God.
Uphold me according to your promise, that I may live,
and let me not be put to shame in my hope!
Hold me up, that I may be safe
and have regard for your statutes continually!

You spurn all who go astray from your statutes,

for their cunning is in vain.

All the wicked of the earth you discard like dross,

therefore I love your testimonies.

My flesh trembles for fear of you,

and I am afraid of your judgments.

I have done what is just and right;

do not leave me to my oppressors.

Give your servant a pledge of good;

let not the insolent oppress me.

My eyes long for your salvation

and for the fulfillment of your righteous promise.

Deal with your servant according to your steadfast love,

and teach me your statutes.

I am your servant; give me understanding,

that I may know your testimonies!

It is time for the Lord to act,

for your law has been broken.

Therefore I love your commandments

above gold, above fine gold.

Therefore I consider all your precepts to be right;

I hate every false way."

Psalm 119:113-128

Read Psalm 119:113-128, twice daily

Summary: This passage expresses that a deep reliance on God's word is a source of hope, wisdom, and guidance. The psalmist describes God as a refuge and shield, emphasizing trust in His promises. These verses contrast the wicked, who stray from God's laws, with the faithful, who love and follow them. He prays for deliverance, wisdom, and understanding, declaring a love for God's commandments above material wealth.

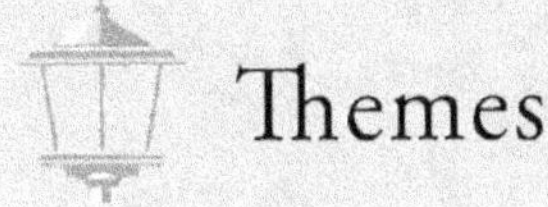 # Themes

Obedient believers:

- View God as their protector, a place of safety in times of trouble.

- Love the Word of God and value it more than material riches.

- Can distinguish between those who follow God's commands and those who do not.

- Ask for discernment and wisdom to follow God's precepts.

- Grieve over those who ignore God's law, showing a zeal for righteousness.

 # Questions for Reflection

Please list five qualities these verses reflect about God.

1.

2.

3.

4.

5.

How can you view God as your refuge and shield in difficult times?

____

____

____

____

____

Do you value God's Word above worldly possessions and personal desires? If so, what can you do to ensure this remains true in the future? If not, how can you make God's Word more valuable to you?

____

____

____

____

In what ways can you grow in your understanding and application of Scripture?

____

____

____

____

What steps can you take to align your heart more closely with God's commandments?

____

____

____

____

Psalm 119:129-144

"Your testimonies are wonderful;
therefore my soul keeps them.
The unfolding of your words gives light;
it imparts understanding to the simple.
I open my mouth and pant,
because I long for your commandments.
Turn to me and be gracious to me,
as is your way with those who love your name.
Keep steady my steps according to your promise,
and let no iniquity get dominion over me.

Redeem me from man's oppression,

that I may keep your precepts.

Make your face shine upon your servant,

and teach me your statutes.

My eyes shed streams of tears,

because people do not keep your law.

Righteous are you, O Lord,

and right are your rules.

You have appointed your testimonies in righteousness

and in all faithfulness.

My zeal consumes me,

because my foes forget your words.

Your promise is well tried,

and your servant loves it.

I am small and despised,

yet I do not forget your precepts.

Your righteousness is righteous forever,

and your law is true.

Trouble and anguish have found me out,

but your commandments are my delight.

Your testimonies are righteous forever;

give me understanding that I may live."

Psalm 119:129-144

Read Psalm 119:129-144, twice daily

Summary: The psalmist expresses deep reverence for God's commandments, describing them as wonderful and full of light. He longs for greater understanding and recognizes that obedience to God's statutes brings wisdom and righteousness. He Pleads for God's guidance, mercy, and protection in the face of trouble and oppression. Despite difficulties, he finds joy and life in God's law, affirming its eternal righteousness while expressing grief over those who disregard it.

# Themes

Obedient believers:

- Value God's statutes as wonderful, giving light and wisdom for daily life decisions.

- Have a deep desire to grow in knowledge and obedience to God's commands.

- Seek God's grace and protection amidst hardship.

- Believe God's commands are just, trustworthy, and bring life even in suffering.

- Believe God's word is a source of delight, stability, and joy.

 # Questions for Reflection

Please list five qualities these verses reflect about God.

1.

2.

3.

4.

5.

Do you view God's Word as wonderful and life-giving? How does it affect your daily life?

____

____

____

____

____

How can you cultivate a deeper hunger for understanding and obeying Scripture?

____

____

____

____

In what ways do you seek God's mercy and guidance during difficult times?

How does recognizing the righteousness of God's law impact your daily decisions?

Do you find joy in obedience, even when faced with trials? How does obedience to God's Word supply you with joy when facing trials?

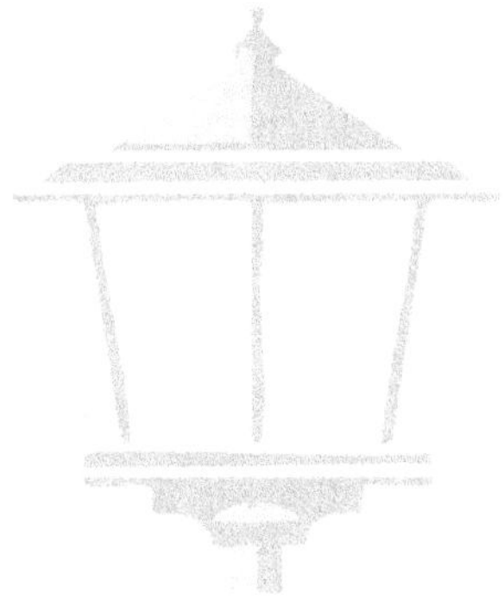

Psalm 119:145-160

"With my whole heart I cry; answer me, O Lord!
I will keep your statutes.
I call to you; save me,
that I may observe your testimonies.
I rise before dawn and cry for help;
I hope in your words.
My eyes are awake before the watches of the night,
that I may meditate on your promise.
Hear my voice according to your steadfast love;
O Lord, according to your justice give me life.

They draw near who persecute me with evil purpose;

they are far from your law.

But you are near, O Lord,

and all your commandments are true.

Long have I known from your testimonies

that you have founded them forever.

Look on my affliction and deliver me,

for I do not forget your law.

Plead my cause and redeem me;

give me life according to your promise!

Salvation is far from the wicked,

for they do not seek your statutes.

Great is your mercy, O Lord;

give me life according to your rules.

Many are my persecutors and my adversaries,

but I do not swerve from your testimonies.

I look at the faithless with disgust,

because they do not keep your commands.

Consider how I love your precepts!

Give me life according to your steadfast love.

The sum of your word is truth,

and every one of your righteous rules

endures forever."

Psalm 119:145-160

Read Psalm 119:145-160, twice daily

Summary: The psalmist cries out to God in prayer, seeking His help and salvation while committing to obey His commandments. He gets up early and meditates on God's Word throughout the night, demonstrating unwavering devotion. Despite facing persecution from the wicked, he finds hope in God's promises and acknowledges His steadfast love. He appeals to God's justice and mercy, affirming that His word is eternal and trustworthy.

 # Themes

Obedient believers:

- Cry out to God with deep desperation seeking His help and deliverance.

- View scripture as a constant source of strength, hope, and wisdom.

- Remain confident in God's righteous promises even in the face of persecution.

- Find comfort in the eternal and unchanging nature of God and His word.

- Obey despite difficulties, and have a firm resolve to follow God's laws.

# Questions for Reflection

Please list five qualities these verses reflect about God.

1.

2.

3.

4.

5.

How can you deepen your prayer life and seek God with your whole heart?

____

____

____

____

____

Do you rely on God's Word as your primary source of hope and strength? How can you use this to find comfort when facing difficulties?

____

____

____

____

____

How do you respond to trials or opposition? Do you trust in God's justice for these situations?

How does God's steadfast love encourage you in difficult times?

Psalm 119:161-176

"Princes persecute me without cause,
but my heart stands in awe of your words.
I rejoice at your word
like one who finds great spoil.
I hate and abhor falsehood,
but I love your law.
Seven times a day I praise you
for your righteous rules.
Great peace have those who love your law;
nothing can make them stumble.

I hope for your salvation, O Lord,

and I do your commandments.

My soul keeps your testimonies;

I love them exceedingly.

I keep your precepts and testimonies,

for all my ways are before you.

Let my cry come before you, O Lord;

give me understanding according to your word!

Let my plea come before you;

deliver me according to your word.

My lips will pour forth praise,

for you teach me your statutes.

My tongue will sing of your word,

for all your commandments are right.

Let your hand be ready to help me,

for I have chosen your precepts.

I long for your salvation, O Lord,

and your law is my delight.

Let my soul live and praise you,

and let your rules help me.

I have gone astray like a lost sheep; seek your servant,

for I do not forget your commandments."

Psalm 119:161-176

Read Psalm 119:161-176, twice daily

Summary: In this final portion, the psalmist expresses deep reverence for God's Word despite facing persecution from powerful enemies. He rejoices in God's law, viewing it as a priceless treasure, and praises Him for His righteous judgments. Acknowledging the peace and security that come from loving God's commands, he also pleads for deliverance and renewal. The psalm concludes with a humble confession of human weakness, comparing himself to a lost sheep and asking God to seek and save him.

 ## Themes

Obedient believers:

- Value Scripture more than worldly riches and find immense joy in its truth.

- Persevere despite opposition from rulers and those in power, remaining steadfast in their faith.

- Experience profound peace through their love for God's law and obedience.

- Openly acknowledge their need for God's help and deliverance through salvation.

- Humbly confess their weakness and their need for God's guidance and help.

 # Questions for Reflection

Please list five qualities these verses reflect about God.

1.

2.

3.

4.

5.

Do you treasure God's Word as a source of joy and guidance in your life? How does the truth of scripture provide you joy?

____

____

____

____

____

How do you respond to challenges or opposition to your faith?

____

____

____

____

____

In what ways do you experience peace through obedience to God?

Are you fully relying on God for deliverance in difficult times? If not, what can you do to ensure you will in the future?

How can you acknowledge your weaknesses and seek God's guidance more earnestly?

Conclusion

I hope this book has been a blessing in your walk with God through the daily challenges of life. Scripture makes it clear that each day will be filled with trouble, but the suffering here cannot compare to the glory that awaits in the place God has prepared for His people. May this resource serve as a reminder in those moments when the accuser tempts you to doubt the faithfulness of our loving God.

In a world that often turns to therapies and pharmaceuticals to cope with life's challenges, we must constantly remember that God has declared His Word sufficient, providing us with all we need for life and godliness.

My prayer is that this workbook will, increase your faith and trust in God's providential care for His children, and above all, exalt God in your thinking to the position He alone deserves. He is God and there is no other.

About the Author

Ron Wolfe serves as a pastor at Redemption Hill Church in Kingsford, MI, where he helps shepherd this congregation with a commitment to their spiritual growth. Holding degrees from Cairn University, Palmer Seminary, and Masters University, Ron understands theology and biblical teaching. His status as a certified member and Fellow with the Association of Certified Biblical Counselors (ACBC) reflects his commitment to biblical counseling. Ron provides biblical counseling to his community, aiming to help individuals navigate life's challenges by applying biblical principles. Ron and his wife Joan have been married for nearly six decades. They have four grown and married children and thirteen grandchildren. Ron's hobbies include golfing, watching Penn State and Pittsburgh Steeler football, and New York Yankee baseball.